THE PORTAGE POETRY SERIES

SERIES TITLES

No Trouble Staying Awake
Teresa J. Scollon

Flu Season
Katie Kalisz

Users with Access: New and Selected Poems
Brandon Krieg

Dining on Salt: Four Seasons of Septets
Wayne Lee

Torrential
Jayne Marek

Another Native Tongue
Susan Riley Clarke

Catch & Release
Lauren Crawford

Steelhead
Lauren K. Carlson

The Coronation of the Ghost
Benjamin Gantcher

The Stone Tries to Understand the Hands
Susannah Sheffer

Red Camaro
Dwaine Rieves

Where Babies Come From
Ori Fienberg

Cuttings
Hannah Dow Kombiyil

Forgive the Animal
Sarah Pape

Love as Invasive Species
Ellen Kombiyil

They Were Horrible Cooks
Allison Whittenberg

The New Life
Wendy Wisner

Restoring Prairie
Margaret Rozga

Table with Burning Candle
Julia Paul

A Bright Wound
Sarah A. Etlinger

The Velvet Book
Rae Gouirand

Listening to Mars
Sally Ashton

Glitter City
Bonnie Jill Emanuel

The Trouble with Being a Childless Only Child
Michelle Meyer

Happy Everything
Caitlin Cowan

Dear Lo
Brady Bove

Sadness of the Apex Predator
Dion O'Reilly

New Wilderness
Jenifer DeBellis

Fulgurite
Catherine Kyle

The Body Is Burden and Delight
Sharon White

Bone Country
Linda Nemec Foster

Not Just the Fire
R.B. Simon

Monarch
Heather Bourbeau

The Walk to Cefalù
Lynne Viti

The Found Object Imagines a Life: New and Selected Poems
Mary Catherine Harper

Naming the Ghost
Emily Hockaday

Mourning
Dokubo Melford Goodhead

Messengers of the Gods: New and Selected Poems
Kathryn Gahl

After the 8-Ball
Colleen Alles

Careful Cartography
Devon Bohm

Broken On the Wheel
Barbara Costas-Biggs

Sparks and Disperses
Cathleen Cohen

Holding My Selves Together: New and Selected Poems
Margaret Rozga

Lost and Found Departments
Heather Dubrow

Marginal Notes
Alfonso Brezmes

The Almost-Children
Cassondra Windwalker

Meditations of a Beast
Kristine Ong Muslim

No Trouble Staying Awake

The deep balance that characterizes these poems—a powerful sense of this but also that, a refusal to simplify and reduce the foreseen and the unforeseen—has a very particular, unforgettable stamp to it. Patiently pondering the ways of our being here and then our leaving here, Teresa Scollon welcomes our vulnerabilities, one outcome of which, however much a long shot, is poetry. As her poems recognize—among many matters—spiders, parents, grief, dogs, geraniums, love, sparrows, and terrible stories, they insist on the genuineness of earthly ties. We say "real" sometimes and sometimes we believe it, but Teresa Scollon engages the dicey gravity of the real in poem after poem. She wears her honesty lightly. This is an outstanding collection.

—BARON WORMSER
author of *The History Hotel*

Teresa Scollon's poems are rooted. I say there's nothing more valuable in the world. King Kong's coming for the child lying in bed at night, waiting for the huge world to get her. The snapper managing to climb out of the heavy dark of the crock. You feel the fierce protective love for earth's creatures. And the care and skill and humor. It's all about seeing and being seen. When the minister bends down to the child, "the world has opened and without warning / and you are real and standing in the center of its blossom." These poems matter.

—FLEDA BROWN
author of *Flying Through a Hole in the Storm*

No Trouble Staying Awake

poems

Teresa J. Scollon

CORNERSTONE PRESS
UNIVERSITY OF WISCONSIN-STEVENS POINT

Cornerstone Press, Stevens Point, Wisconsin 54481
Copyright © 2025 Teresa J. Scollon
www.uwsp.edu/cornerstone

Printed in the United States of America by
Point Print and Design Studio, Stevens Point, Wisconsin

Library of Congress Control Number: 2025932483
ISBN: 978-1-960329-89-9

Cornerstone Press titles are produced in courses and internships offered by the
Department of English at the University of Wisconsin–Stevens Point.

DIRECTOR & PUBLISHER   EXECUTIVE EDITORS
Dr. Ross K. Tangedal   Jeff Snowbarger, Freesia McKee

EDITORIAL DIRECTOR   SENIOR EDITOR
Brett Hill   Ellie Atkinson

PRESS STAFF
Eva Nielsen, Sophie McPherson, Ava Willett, Madison Schultz, Paige Biever,
Autumn Vine

In gratitude for this beautiful world, all its living things, and all the people who care for it.

CONTENTS

I.

II.

III.

No act of kindness, no matter how small, is ever wasted.
—Aesop

There's only one rule that I know of, babies—
God damn it, you've got to be kind.
—Kurt Vonnegut, *God Bless You, Mr. Rosewater*

I.

King Kong

I was seven: just old enough to buy, if I wanted,
a bottle of pop and hold it carefully, not spilling,
while King Kong peered into the windows of a tall building

and Mr. Hawkins patrolled the aisle with his flashlight,
keeping an eye on us kids at the Saturday matinee.
I was there with my friend Michelle. After the movie,

outside it was snowing and near-dusk, and the cars
on Main Street had their wipers going and the street
was slush. We looked both ways and crossed

to the Western Auto hardware, to see Michelle's mom.
I remember the humming lights and the squeak
of the wooden floor and her mother smiling down.

Everything around me said: *This is a good place.*
We keep an eye on things here.
                                        Except at night

when it was only me, lying terrified and awake
in the dark next to my sleeping little sister,
waiting for King Kong to rise just beyond

my mother's handmade curtains. I knew how
to cross the street, how to hold a baby, how
to greet a strange dog. I had a plan for escaping

fire, for waking my brothers and sisters to come
with me. But what would I do when the world
came for me—huge, rough, and sick with longing?

Fire in the House: A Quarantine Poem

After the painting Apartment with Fireplace *by Brian Iler*

At three in the morning, the fireplace
is cold. All matter is made of molecules

and atoms which are always in motion:
translation, rotation, vibration. Motion

creates heat. At three in the morning
my continuous translation of what is, what

was, what could be, is at fever pitch.
I can't sleep. Roll out the yoga mat

to direct this motion into attention, intention.
I can tell you the notion of an indoor fireplace

came with invasion: William the Conqueror.
That was a bloody time. But we got fireplaces

and a grand language out of it. Conduction
is the movement of heat by direct contact:

French with Anglo-Saxon with the priests' Latin.
We can say things in English no one else

can say. So why don't we? Heat spreads:
fires, murders, and lies. The heat radiates:

travels through empty space to reach me and
I feel it. The fireplace says we think we can

regulate fire, domesticate the perilous,
the bloody and indecent maw of history. Here

we are, living with danger in the house. It's said
when large numbers of molecular bonds act

in unison they can make a strong contributory
effect—change the ambient, the vibe. I am just one,

awake and alone in the wee hours. All I have is science.
I'm counting on the strength of the average bond.

The Snapper

In memory of R. Ninomiya

In the long green days of summer
my grandfather caught a snapping turtle
whose feet were as big as his hands.
He stowed it in a heavy crock by the door,
lidded with a thick plate and heavy stone,
and went to bed dreaming of soup.
In the morning the crock was empty
under its plate and stone. The turtle
was gone.

For all we know, it's living still, all
weight and plate and cutting beak,
trudging again the slick bottoms
or lying under the mud in the pond,
snaking its long neck up like a snorkel.
Caught by its relentless nature
and freed also. Think of it encased
in that ceramic tomb. Just another
egg to break out of, maybe. The same
scrabble up slippery sides. The same
imperative. The weight of the lid
on its back, moving backwards
along the carapace, tipping as the turtle
clambered up and out, clattering back
into place over emptiness, while the turtle—
who survived the dinosaurs,
the meteorite and nuclear winter,
my grandfather's dinner plans,
that long moment when you're caught
and held by the wicked and the bad,
hope sealed off, when you
are meant to only wait and tremble—
the turtle worked its slow magic:
Move, move, against the heavy dark.

Sparrow Sonnets

1.

A sparrow hunched, stunned, in the other lane,
holding its tiny self close and still. What
had happened? As we passed in my car—
slowly, I swear I was driving slowly, I saw
that bird sitting there—I passed it, well clear
of it, then heard a light thunk on the rear
of the car. We looked back in the mirror.
Was that the bird? That new lump in the street?
No other cars in the road. Nothing else
to hurt it. We circled back, but a gull
had seen it, flew down to inspect, then rose
with its prize: brown feathers trailing blood.
I was driving my friend to the clinic—
wanting to help care for the world in this way.

2.

There are so many ways to care for the world.
At the hospital, we walked labyrinths
of halls. My friend said they're designed this way
so that if one part burns or is blown up,
there'll be a safe ward somewhere. Separations
within the whole. I dropped her off, circled
back later to find her still waking, shaky.
A nurse had given her a bad IV,
pumped anesthetic into her arm. It grew
hard and painful, but the nurse denied it,
said, *Oh no, you're just nervous.* Only when
my friend did not fall asleep on schedule
did the doctor come to see what was wrong.
What hurt most was how the nurse turned away.

3.

What hurts most is how we turn away.
People do this sometimes, like when my friend

saw a German Shepherd hit once, two times,
on a busy street. No one stopped. Panicked,
she looked for a place to pull over, parked,
ran back to the dog, which had hoisted itself
out of the street. It lay under a tree
in spasms. If she'd known it was dying
she wouldn't have run away for a phone.
She would have held it, quiet, stroking it,
as it passed. Years later she's still telling
this story. Yesterday I saw some geese
trying to cross that street. No one would stop.
To stop what's in motion takes such courage.

4.
To stop what's in motion does take courage.
Take trains. Once a train I rode halted mid-
route for something official, then lingered.
It was a summer Sunday, the sun shone
on the prairie grasses, the train panted
in place. The conductor, flustered, explained
he was trying to coax a dog, a beauty,
from under the train. It was frightened now,
wouldn't come out. It belonged to someone.
He asked for patience. *Please.* We moved forward
to watch through the open doors. One man complained
loudly. *Ridiculous*, he said. He had a schedule
to keep. *Just a dog,* he said. *Run it over.*
I was angry: what kind of beast was he?

5.
Don't you sometimes wonder?
We have so many fears and evils:
cruelty, slaughter, denial, rage. When
there are animals like whales, who live by
hearing, who pitch themselves onto beaches
in despair when they lose their way, their ears.
Elephants stand by their lost ones to grieve;

the spider I roused last night clutched her eggs—
a magnificent orb of gray and white—
tightly in her jaws. We think we know all
there is worth knowing, while around us,
animals live small brave lives. On YouTube,
in Chile, a little brown dog dodges cars
to tug his injured friend off the highway.

6.
What it takes to save a friend in danger
was the theme when the visiting Nigerian bishop
said Mass. The Church holds the world in its old
hands. The bishop told us Muslim youth burned
fifty churches, bombed the cathedral. Terrible,
of course. He asked for our help. But then,
to unify us, he warned that all Muslims
will Islamize the world, which opposes
the Church's plan to Christianize the world.
There are many Muslims in Detroit, he said.
Beware. I do believe he believed himself.
Helping us, he said, *will help you; we are one
in God's love and mercy.* But who is we?
What is mercy? When he finished, people clapped.

7.
Mercy. Is that what made the people clap?
Or was it war? We pump our fists in air,
we like to win, to beat things, to be best.
At a friend's cabin on a quiet cove,
teenage boys come from across the lake
to smoke dope in their boats, out of the view
of their parents. They rev their engines
and race in tight circles, waves battering
the "No Wake" and "Keep the Peace" signs,
the loons and beavers that live here. The only way
to scare off the boys is to stand naked
on the end of the dock, our aging bodies
saying: *one day you will be as soft as we.
Tenderness is all we have.*

The Drugmobile: a Short History

My father's white Bronco, young and untiring
as he, which did the heavy work: hauling
cattle chutes down gravel roads; clambering

into the fields for a downed heifer; out late
for emergencies and up with the early milkers
until it caught fire at the stoplight

in the middle of town and that was the end
of it. Then a series of family cars, used up
or outgrown by his family and now his:

the red Olds; the station wagon with fake wood
panels on the sides, a bucket of slop in the back
for the pigs and the passenger side door that swung

open during left turns as he headed out of town
on a call. Or the old van, with the key broken
in the ignition, started by a screwdriver

lying ready on the console; and finally
the sturdy pickup, truly his, which he nursed
and charged each night in winter,

with a box of sliding drawers he built from plywood
and painted white, which held ropes and tools
for the muscle work of cutting horns or pulling calves.

Whatever the vehicle, best watch for needles
in the seat before sitting down, syringes
in their plastic packages, the bright dust of road

and the sharp, acrid smell of medicine.
His left arm bent and resting in the open
window, finding his way around the grid

of country roads, picking up milk
and tooling up the Seeger Street hill
on the way home, not too worried

about staying inside the center line.
His wheels, his calling, pack of gum
in the ashtray, rolling through planted rows

of green and gold, the garden that is the Thumb
in summer, treating animals, talking politics
with farmers. His shelter in the bitter cold,

as he worked the knots out of a piece of line
with stiff fingers, muttering *this damned business!*
while a heifer labored in a loafing shed.

Finally, in broad summer, between chemo rounds,
parked on a grassy hill, there for a simple job:
castrating a couple of calves—he took a chill,

got himself to the truck, hauled himself
into the passenger seat and huddled there,
shivering, under his coat, under my coat,

under a blanket we found, while the heater blazed
and roared, gushing hot air, the labor and din
of machinery he'd soon be leaving behind.

To You on the Other Side

for my father

This morning, on the viburnum, clusters
of tiny insects, packed so close the stem
appeared brown, and over the bugs clambered
a few brown ants, touching them with feelers—

exploring, or maybe tending the bugs—
and me, trying to get a better look,
pulling one leaf out by its tip so far
an ant crawled over to investigate.

And over me, maybe, something watching,
Coast Guard recruits steering their choppers;
farther, satellites blinking, peering down.
Beyond, maybe God, maybe guardian

angels. I hope so. And you, who I still miss,
still call on. Are you there? Can you see me?

After Perfection

1.

A woman retires, moves to the north,
to a house on a small wild lake. Annoyed
by the free creatures living under her dock,

a mink and her babies, their mess of crayfish shells,
she has them shot as they drowse in their nest.
Where is Dante when you need him?

He'd devise her perfect and deserved hell—
a cement box to live in, which she cleans
and cleans and cleans and cleans, never

recognizing it as hell. To her
the lake is a picture postcard
where nothing stirs and nothing will.

2.

The full moon, round as round can be,
looks down at me through my window.
There will always be murder, it says.

Pity the woman empty of wonder.
She does not know where she is,
pacing her quarters, a Lady MacBeth

scrubbing her floors, scrubbing her hands
of her dark business. But I mourn the lost ones,
the rippling beauty of wild, the she-creature

that brought life into the world
and harmed no one. Let my poem
find the woman in her warm bed,

let her feel its cold steel on her forehead.

Vagrants

or accidentals, who stray
far outside their expected
range, like Santa Claus

marooned in the Florida Keys—
impossible not to spot
in that red suit—or Hmong refugees

arriving to the leafless trees
of Minnesota in winter.
They are often solitary, say,

as you might be lying alone
in a hospital bed, and they may
be nervous, exhausted, blown

off course and hungry, thinking
This is not my beautiful house.
The key is the distance

from the original course. Like a parrot
calcified as a Paris gargoyle:
it's very far from home.

But a Michigan Bean Queen
in Great Plains cattle country is only
a train ride away. And it's all

still flattish land. Boys climbing
trees look like strange birds
but it's a temporary condition;

what happens if you leave
town, go to college, change
partners or expectations?

The arrival of vagrant visitors
can cause great excitement
among the flock, or the neighborhood

block party, where everyone wonders
about the man camping at the park
pavilion: Is this a precursor

to colonization? And what created
this abnormality—wind or predators,
unfavorable climate or scarcity

of food? Navigation gone
gollywhompus—it happens. But
what if it's the strays who save us,

as in a mongrel dog, a kind passerby,
a floating male maintaining
genetic diversity on the sly?

Vagrants, rarities—it's not
really about the bird, is it? It's how
you feel about the bird.

II.

Easter

There is your world and there is the world above you,
which is yours but not yours, a feeling reinforced
by the wide brim of your new hat. You are all dressed up
so God can see you. There are your feet in shiny
black shoes, lacy white anklets your mother
folded just so, your blue coat, and white gloves
holding the little wicker purse you've been given to keep,
its clasp you can open and close, its pink flowers
with their plastic promise of eternal life. Did I mention
that the light is bright and raw? Everything is new
and cold and everyone is happy. Outside the church
you see the slim black legs of Father coming near.
He speaks to your mother, who is holding your hand.
As you tip your head up like a flower finding sun,
you see Father's long lean down from above,
his black shirt, the collar with its snowy lozenge,
the face which seeks you, and finds you,
and looks you in the eye. "Good morning!" he says.
And you will remember this: that he has seen you,
that your world has opened gently and without warning
and you are real and standing in the center of its blossom.

Hard-Boiling Eggs

First you hear the rush of water heating, rattle
of shells against pan. I like how the eggs,

blank, impassive, somehow holy, begin to tremble
and lift off the bottom, like little dirigibles,

edible and sincere, riding the currents, the roiling
boiling water. Their time in the fire is strictly

timed, their baptism in cold as long as it takes.
Now they rest, quiet and cooling.

I inscribe the shell with felt-tip pen—a custom
I learned from a great-aunt: big black Xs,

the mark of the unlettered that says: this is me
signing this, the original signature that is the same

for everybody, and also the symbol of the Christ
and the cruelty he endured on the cross,

a reminder of our darkness, how part of us
is boiling inside, poking out sharpnesses.

But eggs are mute imperturbable parcels,
the shell perfectly fitted to what's inside:

potential child swaddled in slippery brine,
now cooked and opaque, digestible,

a sacrifice marked and stored in the fridge
in humble cardboard, a gift of life again.

Extravagance

Mamie the White Oak is having sex well
into her eighties. She's been at it for days, and now
in the afterglow, she's letting fall
curtains of catkins, spent strings of flowers,
blanketing the streets with brown bouclé.

"Heaven's sake, Mamie," says I, "We're covered
down here." Mamie's a slow talker.
"Well…" is about all I get out of her,
and even that's imaginary.

I gather up the flowers in handfuls, arrange them
in thick cowl-like scarves around my seedlings.
They're like my mother's mohair shrug; she sewed it
herself to wear to dances, snug in homespun glamour.

I examine a catkin more closely: such tiny flowers!
Two could dance on the head of a pin, and each the site
of some vegetable joy, meaning a big girl like Mamie,
with her millions of flowers, must have endless
capacity for delight. Pity all the people inside

watching "Bachelorette," hoping for some wild stuff.
I give the oak a pat, look up into her branches,
and it occurs to me that Mamie has probably known,
if you catch my drift, trees from clear across town.

"Mamie, you devil," I say, but she makes no reply.
She's resting, or maybe focusing all her attention
on one last teensiest flower that's just finishing up.

Factory Job

There was the coming and going, gliding in
on my bicycle as the farm women pulled up
in their trucks, punching our time cards in the early

cool, passing onto the floor where we became
moving parts among moving parts, trained,
broken in, timed. All women, except

for the foreman and the boy my age who came
around with a wheelbarrow or a broom
and trays of throttle bodies. All women

at the drill presses. *That's right*, said Dad.
*Women have smaller hands, they don't have
these meat hooks*, and he held up his hands.

But I had watched his hands, large and deft,
reaching into an opened animal to find the uterus,
sewing it closed again, or fashioning a cast.

He'd taught me to hold a small animal, to pull
both ears back with one hand to keep the face
taut and the animal distracted while he

inserted a needle or a thermometer.
And my mother had taught me the sewing
machine, and the piano teacher wrote

in my notebook every week: Practice
R.H. scales and L.H. scales and then
R.H. and L.H. together. At the factory

stand facing the drill press. With L.H,
reach and take a throttle body from the tray,
fit it into the fittings on the press; it will

turn and latch like a bobbin in its case.
And meanwhile R.H. is pulling the drill lever
down and toward you, just the right amount

of pressure, just the right speed to glide
the bit down into and back up. L.H. releases
the throttle body from the fitting, passes it

into R.H. which places the body into the tray
to the right while L.H. reaches for another
from the left. Body as piston and wheel.

Pink lubricant running over the fittings,
under my latex gloves, soaking my jeans.
The heat. A rough fan near a broken window.

No long thought; just fitting bodies into narrow
slices of time and place, trying to catch the rhythm
of a machine running at full boil. At lunch,

a sandwich in my paper bag, seated at long
tables with the other women. I was the young one,
the college student, marked and shy.

Outside the summer bloomed and faded.
Work was our life but not our lives. Our lives were
elsewhere. At 3:30, the farm women got into their trucks

and drove off. I took up my bicycle for the ride home
in the heat, my jeans as soaked and heavy
as in the pool at swimming class, learning how

to survive when I was weighted down,
as heavy as possible, that same feeling. Clammy
T-shirt, the absence of thought, the dull press
of my legs pushing up the grinding hill.

Cabbages

Behind the garage, cabbages rot
in the ground, planned luminaries
of the garden, their collars spread

all Elizabethan, purple and green.
I planted them in rings, thought I'd
tend their wild verdancy.

I didn't count on summer's hot length,
the stamina required to see them
through, the shabbiness of poor soil:

sand shot through with road's fallout.
But they survived, raising heavy heads
up toward the power lines. Now

wild rabbits have feasted here,
the white hearts of cabbage torn open
to November sky, outer leaves

blackened and slimed by frost.
Their odor rises. I should be ashamed:
my women taught me better thrift.

Years ago, my grandmother sat one day
in my parents' kitchen, peeling
withered apples for a pie, rolling flat

with a rolling pin washed pieces
of used aluminum foil—the ancient
women's work of piecing together

something out of small nothings.
She'd left a job, the city she loved,
to follow her husband to a washed-out

farm in 1944, the only woman
on that country road to have known
streetcars, a flush toilet, who learned

to can and salvage, bound to her man
in unhappy truce. She learned her ropes.
That day I was leaving my first love. In his car

we drove around the four-mile square,
the fields cleared and empty. We believed
we were the only two in the world,

our love the only unsalvageable
love. We wept and circled everything
we'd known. It could not hold me.

Back at the house, my grandmother
gave us soup made from scraps and bones.
He found it good. Was that the moment

I left all love behind? Now tired
of wandering, I wonder. Truth is,
I had no patience for snares. And now

the time is past when I could make something
of this garden. I will have to give it up,
prepare the ground for winter. Better to leave

it to the rabbits, the one wildness
in this settled place, who grow lush
on what they steal, blasting open

the closed dense circuits of cabbage,
living on their own wary terms,
the neighborhood cats hot on their trails.

Big Dog

Probably you've come across my mark
around here. That's me. Thirty-five pounds

of Big Dog. Here is my chest. Here
is my head. Probably you will want to touch

me. I live here with Her and I'm in charge
of certain things. The yard. The bastard squirrels.

The world comes to me through the air
and I check it for things I know: animals, food,

strangeness. I have my dolls on the side.
When I give you my special look, you'll know

you are my doll. Once you find a good
thing, stick with it. The sofa. The pee spot.

The First Doll. I never waver. There's a way
to do things. To make things nice. I know

what to do. On the leash, how fast
She walks. In the morning, never bark

in Her ear. Go into the next room to bark.
When invited into the Bed, make a little

fuss. Give Her your chest. Dolls like that.
When She wavers or cries, lean, get close.

You have to let a doll know
where love will come from.

I Don't Know, What Do *You* Wanna' Do?

The point is to have faith. Like the Baptist kids
on Mondays, getting all that Sunday evangelizing

out of their systems, chasing us Catholic kids around
the playground, waving their little bibles, pointing

to passages proving we were going to hell, pitting
their belief against—what? The Catholic kids:

disparate and unorganized, saved and mostly unaware
of it, wrestling privately with our anxieties,

watched, and maybe watched over, by our God
and angels and saints and what have you, all of us

running around on a cement we called tarvy, skinning
our knees on the logic of the time: hold a hard surface

under these kids so when they fall they will feel it.
Kids pitching themselves off the high slide into

senselessness. Forming our letters within grids of solid
and dotted lines. Everything had rules, even explorations:

boys piling on the merry-go-round, shouting in giddy
unison, *Girls push! Girls push!* Religion divided us,

stopped all conversation. What if I'd stopped running
to say, *Fine, save me. I'm spiritual putty in your hands.*

What if salvation leapt from kid to kid like a wildfire,
classrooms alight with the Holy Spirit? What's the fire drill

for that? But no, that's not how it was. We Catholics had no
easy retort. Our hell was nuanced, tiered, more complicated

than they knew. We may have been doomed, but those
Baptists were a pack of fools. By Tuesday we were friends

again, trading the refrain: *I don't know, what do you wanna' do?*—
trusting the company of all of us who didn't know ourselves,

opening to the wishes of the other—that beautiful leap—
and in the face of everything we were being taught,

the young hope that something good might happen
between us, and all we had to do was ask.

Shame and Something Else

Someone shot the beagle at close range
        with a crossbow, the arrow stuck crosswise
                through its body, just under the spine.
    But a boy found the dog stumbling in the woods
and brought it in, worked off the vet bill in barter.
        Someone left the cattle to starve in the barn,
                standing locked in their stanchions. Someone
        gave the six-pound puppy a good quart of beer
            for fun. A cat prowled the barn
                  with a loop of intestine hanging out.
        Someone left the dachshund in the cold garage
                for three days, trying to birth its dead pup,
            until the stink could not be ignored.
Someone put out poison, aimed his truck at the turtle in the road.
        Someone beat the draft horse with a loose board
            ripped off the fence in anger.
    An angry guard shoves a ragged letter under a cell door.
                    But the letter comes. Someone's
    ears are filled with the speech of birds. Someone
   dreams of flying. Someone shows another
    how to bathe a child. A small dog snoozes
  in the sun beside a door. Someone stands
   in the yard shading her eyes with her hand, counting
 birds. Someone tries to patch
   things up. For shame. For something else.
Someone holds the door. Someone
        takes a piece of paper, carefully
            picks up a spider, sets it outside.

III.

Geopolitics, Stateside

I have been too lenient, letting the dogs climb
onto the couch, where they love to straddle and shout
at squirrels, at animals walking by. Hey, I say,

knock it off. How about a little live and let live
around here? Real Americans, these two, lovers
of comfort, lovers of love. Ferocious players.

I wonder at their teeth, their power. Surely
they smell my blood beneath this thin sheath
of skin. Amazing that they let me live.

But this easy living has gone too far. Everywhere
the odor of dog. The couch is stained by clots
of dirt from claws or possibly rectum, grime

from their oily coats. It must be cleaned. I find
the cushions I lean against have no structure: inside
the cover just loose green fuzz. Somewhere someone

makes a living making this stuff—Is it a child?
So much I don't know. I vacuum up grit
and acorn shards beneath the cushions,

and note the frame: steel visible under a thin scrim,
coiled and ready to spring. Meanwhile one dog
is giving the other the stink-eye who erupts

in noise. Somehow I must manage this. How
much will have to be done again, over and over?
Consider the washing machine, which does what it does,

like a man focused on one idea only. Things come out clean
but threadbare and shaken. One dog sheds like crazy,
the other's so greasy she leaves streaks on the walls.

They had to be trained not to shit in the house,
that their house is my house, too. Every once in a while
there's a new regime around here, say, after watching

Cesar Milan on the TV, but who can focus on status
all the time? It's an alpha concern when there is other work
to be done. Anyway, we live as a pack here. When I sink

onto the couch the dogs press their bodies against my legs,
look into my eyes. We are here, they say. Now.
Message of the bodhisattva. Not the moment

to introduce new rules. After all, they are perpetually
who they are. I count on them to keep me safe.
So I work at the stains on the sofa with a washcloth

and a little white soap. The cushion covers go
into the machine on delicate cycle, with extra low
agitation. I am only trying not to destroy

what I have. It is not that it is any less soiled.

Spring

to J.E.

I can't reach
your cool water;
it's so far down.

Ears to stone
I imagine the quiet
kiss of sweet water

against the cool
blunt walls
of this well, think

I smell rain
or spring. And
out here—listen,

new birds are
leaving their broken
shells behind, bees

fatten. Trees
shove pollen
over the sills

of their flowers
and everything
is so thirsty.

Inquiry

how's your water Governor
is it clean does it clear

your clouded mind we see
you're a little shy of the questions

and the cameras and Congress
and the city of Flint and

we're wondering if you're
okay maybe someone's told you

if you close your eyes it's only
a game there's nobody there but

friends or fellow beneficiaries
or you think *you're* the one

who's invisible drawing a magic
cloak over yourself and ballots

and budget bills and pipelines
and lab samples hide-and-seek

from subpoenas maybe that's
the game but this isn't just

a matter of solving a problem
with the pipes Governor no it runs

deeper we wonder what you've been
drinking to acquire this special

blindness all the people and kids
the brown water the tufts of hair

this noise all the anti-everything
is just us Governor who drink water

trying to get your attention
and another thing this silence

is not nothing that's people too
listening and yes apparently

this is going to be a thing
Governor until you see us

clear as water

Cussing

Mouth's rite of passage, like the kiss,
attracts and terrifies, requires practice.

Like spitting seeds at targets—
the aim, the strike, the splatter,

the make-believe that nothing matters.
The mind's a girl who blushes, trills

to vicarious swagger. And now trot in
the sturdy, long-lived quadrupeds of English,

well-travelled, nicked in barfights, sly.
Offering the coarse affection that assures

you there's no better. The kind of guy
your mother hates to see you with,

who takes you for a spin on a rusty
carny ride, with arms flung out and gut

clenched, the thrill of being knocked around
but let off at the end unharmed. It's just a ride.

But then one day the heart is sunk
in disappointment, a trapped bear pacing

in an empty moat, and curse words become
battered stairs headed nowhere, up into soured air;

the clot and litter of jagged bricks left
after a building's fall; old butts reeking

in an ashtray, all bitterness and bawl.

In the Basement at Child and Family Services

Tuesday nights the basement fills for foster parent training.
We come just out of work, pressed for time, before dinner.
We introduce ourselves. *We live in this town. We plan
to adopt. We have our grandbabies now and have to get
certified. I was a foster child myself. I have room.
I have time. There's a child.*
    *

Next to me, a man intently colors in a diagram. He has
the thick body and clothes of a man who works
outside. An earring glints from one ear. When
called on, he nods at his wife, who speaks
for them both. They thought they'd raised theirs, but
the daughter's got so many problems, now
they have her kids. The four-year-old doesn't want
to see his mother though the court requires it. He's mad.
Only four. Now the daughter is pregnant again
by another man. They raised her. *How could
this happen?* We nod. The man does not
look up. He is bright with pain.
    *

They discover I'm a teacher. My lettering
on a chart gives me away. They ask me
about schools. I don't know anything about elementary,
why a teacher would point out a foster kid,
why a teacher would say a child smells.
My students are young adults, some of them
parents already, some of them beginning
another string of lives.
    *

To make a child welcome, find out what kind
of food they like. Make it. Remember
maybe they have just been pulled

out of their home. Remember they are scared.
Remember they are having lots of feelings.
Make a photo album of yourself and your family
and the room that will be theirs. Decide how
to handle food. They might get up in the middle
of the night to find it. They might wet the bed.
Put a plastic protector on the mattress but don't
make a big deal of it. You can't prevent them
from leaving. Remind them if they aren't back
in an hour you have to call the cops.

*

A man there to be a foster parent remembers
his childhood out loud. In his house
there was no food. They were beaten if they made
food. He's strong now, with big arm muscles.
His wife says when he gets cranky, agitated,
she asks him if he is hungry. *That's usually it*,
he says. His voice full of wonder.

*

We have special guests: a man with his two
adopted sons. All three wear a jacket and tie.
The man says when the boys met him
they asked if he would have enough money
for food. His voice cracks. The boys listen
and look at us. The adoption worker
asks the ten-year-old to say how it was when
they met her. The boy says, *We were
at McDonald's. And you said you would find
a nice home for us. And you did.*

*

Stories pile up, flooding the basement.
What it was like to be hungry. Hiding
outside the house. How an uncle
hurt. How an uncle helped. How a boy

knows he can slip the two little ones
into the cabinet before him, so when
they are discovered, he will be pulled out
first; he will take the beating. How the girl
writes a poem to say *I'm in here, Please,*
Don't stop trying. How the boy dragged
from his bed to watch his brother beaten
in the basement will have the harder time
adjusting. How all the stories walk through
the valley of darkness. How children will try
to save each other, how adults try
too, the urge to give and give, to brace
two feet against the rocking boat
of the world to steady it.
                         *

Sometimes I think, when I hear these stories,
[*ropes, irons, cigarettes*] people should not be able
to move like this. We should not be able
to think this up. We should not have
these shoulders and the weight behind them.
We should not have these hands.
                         *

But in the basement, we work. We share one
bathroom, eat Oreos and popcorn for supper. These
are hours of deep water. We're caught
stilled and heavy in our chairs, our hands
in continuous motion. We twist pipe cleaners
into bracelets while we listen. We are so tired.
We have no trouble staying awake.

Kitchen Window

She was unpacking a box from UPS on the kitchen counter—
$400 worth of powders to fight off the cancer—
and I was eating breakfast at the table, after a shower, fueling

for another shift at his bedside in the hospital, just her and me, keeping
vigil there in turns, watching for the tremors that kept coming back.
He lay there beneath words, dreamy, his blue eyes sometimes opening,

his hands reaching out slowly, touching the sides of the bed to test
where he was. When I spoke to him, he looked back the way an infant does,
recognizing only that he belonged to someone and that is why we tried

never to leave him. When she wasn't at the hospital she'd been searching
all hours on the internet for cures, regimens, herbal magic, something,
anything to wedge between him and what was coming.

She set each jar on the counter, wondering how we'd ever get him
to drink this stuff now that he was beyond eating, and I said back—breaking,
I couldn't help it—"I don't want you to put him through anything else."

She stopped, the moment at last landing in her. She looked at the jars
in her hands and I remember it was really her, the one who could see
where she was and what she was doing. She stood with the east light

of February on her face and it was the window over the sink, where
so many times I would see her come during the day to draw a glass of water
from the tap and stand there to drink it and look out, and then leave,

setting the glass down next to the sink. There was always a glass there
for her. This was her neatest gesture, this woman who left a trail of coffee cups
and newspapers and articles torn out of magazines and Kleenex and keys,

who could never find anything, who fretted that she could never find anything,
but she always knew where to find water, coming to the sink like a little bird.
Of all the windows in that house that was her window, where she left

tokens on the sill—a sprig of plant in a glass to take root, or
a half-sucked cough drop, or a single earring—
all the half-lost things she meant to come back for.

I Want to Be Joe Manchin's Momma

I want to be Joe Manchin's momma,
to set myself down at the kitchen table
with a cup of tea and wait until he stumbles

home in the wee hours. My quiet will scare
him so; my mild will make him cringe.
"Is that you, Joe?" I'll say. "Is that *my* Joe?

Who came out my body? The boy *I* raised?
You better set down right now, son,
I hardly recognize you. Look here

at all this money on the table.
I found this in your pants pockets,
doing laundry. That's a *lot* of money, son.

Where'd. You. Get. It. Is this why I fed your
poor departed hard-working daddy beans
instead of meat, when we was saving

to send you to college? All that sacrifice.
Every night. You think about it good now.
So you could go and become a common thief?

And who you been out with so late? Shuffling
into your momma's house at this hour! No,
don't you interrupt me. I don't need an

answer. It was a rhetorical question. You think
I don't know that big word? You going to tell me
you were praying with Jesus in the garden?

You a liar now, too? And aren't you ashamed
of this climate deal. You so big, now, Mr. Senator,
that you don't have to live in this world,

with the birds, and the trees, and the creatures?
This beautiful world that God made for us and gave us
to care for, and is suffering and dying because of the *heat*,

and needs us to take care of it and figure it out
and you just jerking good people around
and you can't do your *job*?

You take this paper, here, and this little pencil.
I sharpened it good while I waited for you.
You set right here and you write an apology

to the people of this world and to God who loves you
and to your momma who loves you despite it all.
And you get up tomorrow and you go straight back

to Washington and you make it right. I'll set the alarm
for six o'clock. I already packed your lunch.
I'll make you some eggs for breakfast."

Corduroy Quilt

After the textile art by Susan Wild Barnard

We have our ways
of fitting together. Peg and groove.
Mortise and tenon. Tender.
Sleeping, we wrap our bones
in another's arms, the warm
ridges of corduroy. Topography
of relation. Heat. Nap.

Valleys between
ridgelines. Each of us a new
whorled. Fingerprints, our ridges,
our badges. Marked. Marking.

It's not always easy.
For example, the hand—spike
of the finger or the raised club
of a fist. Hackles. Bared teeth.
Even eyelashes are tiny
spines. Ribs' rigging,
braided hair. Lock. Unlock.

To corduroy is to form
a road by laying logs transversely.
As a road over swampy ground.
The ground between us.
Whole cloth.

Or holed cloth. Pieces,
punctures, the wounds needling
makes, the effort required
to poke through, stitch together.
Sore thumb and steel thimble,
helmet on the tender finger
ends. Will. See it through.

The existentialists said
no right nor wrong, only choices.
This block or that one. Red
for heart. Brown for earth. Black
for where we came from, where
we're going. Blue for the big sky.

The eye moves in,
     moves out. Close up, the eyes
close. Inside the eyeball, tiny
peaks peek, activate. Even
inside, texture. In other words,

          nothing, nothing, nothing,
is a smooth sea. Deep down,
coral: the calcified palace
of domesticity. How we think
this is it, this will always be it.
Until you scrape your skin
on the bottom, and if a sudden
wave pins you down. Well, then.
Beware

          words, with their cavities
and chasms never kissed by sun,
or the foggy hills of ambiguity.
But then we speak of love.
Rope bridges, spider webs spun
out of miraculous fiber. Honey
pouring out of pores.

          Light falls on this gold—
grain ready for harvest. Yellow dog
snoozing in the sun. Dogs don't worry
about any of this, sleep on the bed
no matter what you say. So many
words but no word for this color:
amber, camel, caramel. Hum.

IV.

Geranium

After the painting by Judy Acha

The unlikely subject. The ordinary. Like the screen
door every morning in the summer. You can hear
from your room upstairs how your father

gets up early, goes into the kitchen to clear his throat
and blow his nose. He honks. He sets the teakettle
on the stove and steps outside to pick up the paper.

The screen door's long creak and slam. He stands
in the early light and looks east where white clouds
gather over the lake. Everyday clouds.

Or your mother out in the yard after supper,
deadheading petunias and geraniums, fingering
the flowers and chatting with Naomi from next door.

Familiar flowers, flowers we don't even see,
like neighbors or clouds or your parents bringing in the mail
every day, setting it on the table and pausing

to let the dog walk by. You drink tea after supper
because your parents did, chatting at the table
after the kids left. Always they shared a teabag:

dunk, dunk. And always they asked you, as you
cleared the table, for a small glass of cool water
and whether there weren't any little cookies left

in the cupboard. The geranium on the porch
saw the sunrise, the sunset, the days lengthen
into these long summer astonishments, evenings

that taste what it would be like to live forever.
When you grow up you will see geraniums for the first time
when you realize what your mother, grandmother knew:

that nothing is so beautiful as red, nothing so real
as the ordinary. A geranium sends its peppery musk
through the window. A dog's barking two streets down,

neighbors calling across the way. Now you are older,
visiting this house. You remember how your father
taught you to pray by kneeling with you

at the foot of the bed. How your mother scrubbed
the floor on her hands and knees. Folding
chairs in the church basement and percolated coffee.

Chocolate cake was chocolate cake—No
death-by-chocolate, no molten lava. Just cake.
For forty-five years your mother got two cups of tea

from every teabag; now she's alone, but there is no way
she'll let any teabag off easy. She saves them
in little saucers on the counter where they dry out.

When she isn't looking, you crumble them into the flowerbeds
like so much ash. Dust to dust. It seems impossible
that your father is dead, that your friends have moved away,

that this long summer evening is not an evening forty years ago.
Look. Isn't this the same geranium? The very same, with its rough pot
and crooked elbows. A modest beauty, a vintage darling

who's aged well. Your skin is alive. You feel the earth under
your bare feet. A dog comes by with its usual habits of love.
Everything is flooded with unending light, the annual gift

of this latitude. You walk in the yard with your widowed mother
and notice another day of ordinary astonishments.
Daystar and birdsong. The light comes and comes and comes.

Supper's over, your father's gone, and the light still comes.
What will you do with all this light? You stand in the yard,
touching everything with your hands and your eyes,

tongue fingering the names of all the things you nearly
forgot, all the first things you ever loved: Mama,
Daddy. Dog. Apple tree. Rose. Geranium.

Marking Hems

to accentuate delicate ankles, the shapely calf, what becomes you.
Stand still on the chair, your mother crouching, pins in her mouth,

measuring the skirt, your body with her eyes, things she has made
and is still perfecting. You are a good girl, she has made certain,

though she hates how you hide behind all that hair. Once, helping
your mother down the gym bleachers you saw how she minced, swung

her hips. Your father first kissed her after she'd fallen down
a flight of stairs in high heels. He ran down and knelt beside her.

They laugh as they tell this story. *Don't you have dances?* they ask.
At home, she trips on the stairs holding a laundry basket and groceries

and whatever needs carrying. He knocks the heels of his hands against
his forehead. *Watch what you're doing*, he pleads. *Twirl*, she says,

so if you should twirl it will be lovely. The skirt falls naturally.
This is a hem: a series of pin pricks, the suggestion of a line,

a subtle hand tucking the thread into and under the fold. Lift
your skirts in your hands to step up stairs. Don't unravel. Remember

a kiss is not a receipt for a hamburger. Leave a generous margin
for future changes of mind. Mark the skirt, pin it. When you are sure,

press firmly. Never let the stitches show.

At Clear Creek

to J.E.

1.
Two days hike down into the Grand Canyon,
rock piled and towering around us. It's not a straight
nor easy path: nine miles of up and down, across
mesas, through passes, through layers of history,
caught in the deep carvings of the Colorado.
On the last descent, stumbling on untrustworthy legs
along a narrow edge of crumbling red Hakatai shale,
I stopped, shaking, at my body's limits. You waited
while I gathered myself, called on my father's name,
remembered his difficult descent. At last we lie
under the sky at the bottom of the canyon, between
the water and the old cottonwoods. Both our fathers,
now dead, taught us to watch the stars, to remember,
to see. Clear Creek warbles in its bed.

The world has moved into shadow; all that remains
is the outline of a world, the buttes are black curtains,
window jambs framing the universe.
Before us, the stars—what we have in common
with the ancients, but which we rarely see, slipping,
as we do, behind our modern scrim of lights.

2.
At the hospital, I kept slipping into the weighted
canyons of sleep, beside my father's bed.
Nine months in, he'd begun to make noises
in the night, testing his voice, his realness.
Three times he called: *Terese? Are you still awake?*
Each time I answered more slowly, less certain.
The hospital at night is another universe,
never silent, but hushed, filled with sounds
that sweep or pulse, the circular whoosh

of floor cleaners, the steady beep of monitors,
green and winking. He was keeping a vigil
over himself, over what was still his body.
I could not stop sleeping. Already we
were like continents shifting apart.

3.
I wake now to stars, a larger comfort.
I did not know I was sleeping. I want to say
how sad it is we are slipping away
from our stars. But I don't feel sad. The age
of the stars, maybe. Even the lost ones
send their light for years and years. We roll
through the universe, naming things to make them
real, calling our own names softly. Maybe the dead,
too, are winking behind the day's light.
The Big Dipper pivots across the sky
all night, tethered to the North Star, the fixed
point of navigation, which tonight
lies out of our view, hidden as it is behind
the buttes, behind the solid earth.

Dung Beetles

navigate by starlight, hugging their wad,
their stash, their futures—is not what I say
to the men moving the couch

while I open and close doors around them
as if I was evolved to do it. They, on the other
hand, have got a strange modern shuffle.

The sofa's from Goodwill, will give us
ease until its season ends and it returns
to Goodwill. In this way, the couch is dung

moving in circles. The house is just
expensive access to ground, the right to plant
flowers, name birds, watch stars through

the empty winter branches. I couldn't
take care of it alone. Good thing
men are so generous with their muscles.

Look at these boys, carrying my shit—
they look so natural. The dung beetles
have been on my mind for a while, charting

their courses by light of the Milky Way,
a fact confirmed by fitting them with little
paper hats to block their view of the sky.

Without their guide they move in tiring
circles, getting nowhere. I empathize; I know
the force of earthly imperative: the couch,

the mortgage I wear like a hat, other worries
that obscure the light. For beetles, single stars
merely confuse; the whole galaxy is needed.

How things fit together, that's what matters—
like the miracle of roofs that hold weight
over our heads while we sleep. Somebody

figured that out and shared. Another
wonder: how we sometimes help each other
find the right road. Once my love drove us

straight through the black night emptiness
of Texas. He pulled over; we got out.
He backed me up against him and held

me close. Look, he said. We looked up.

Stolen Code

for the mRNA vaccine

By now the instructions have been destroyed,
dissolved and dumped with the trash,
as in any spy story,

the ribonucleic messengers expelled
in the nano-balls of lipids they slid
around in. And good

riddance. They were greasy company,
but useful. By now the cells
have all assembled

their spikes, like the cruel gutter
spikes that discourage pigeons,
who by another name

are the doves of peace. Easy for me
to talk of peace, when my role
is merely ceremonial,

parasitical, swanning around above
the neck while the city-state of the body
prepares for siege.

We are creatures of war, meant to survive,
committed right down to the cell.
I am allowed

to think what I like, to siphon energy,
to pretend I know what's going on,
to write odes.

Fall Comes to the Loop

the spring wind must bring them
or else they hatch between glass
and granite the spiders set up shop

in the window thirty floors up
their lives are rich in what
the wind brings them

living head-down as they do
growing fat as legged pancakes
tasting the unlimited

grass of prairies the gleam
and clink of the inner earth
the air itself it is theirs

all summer they build and duel
captains of industry neatly converting
the blood of millions their bellies

bulging in their subtle shirts
in late summer the winds increase
there's no hiding no escape

the spiders are flung to the street
their webs battle-torn banners
flipping heedlessly in wind

everywhere spiders are falling
on the ground I step around
the maimed and crawling

for the gutter their lives
in the air are over
there are birds too lying dead

on the sidewalk who saw the sky
where none existed
a different problem

River, Page

to Y. Thao

1.
Look how you've carried these small bodies
across the ocean. How gently you laid these
children down at the fire where stories are told.

I hear it again: how the choppers lifted
out of Saigon, cut away the desperate arms
and fled, how the Hmong fled in small groups

of families or fighters, trekking across
verdant Laos, leaving behind their ambushed
precious dead as they raced to the Mekong River

and, beyond, to the Thai camps; how one family
came to the river and lashed each adult,
each child, to a bamboo pole fit under

the arms to keep them afloat, tied
everyone together, a string of soft pearls
crossing the animal river; how the parents,

pulling the weight of that chain, began to choke
and falter, began to drown, felt the river
claim them; how the father drowned something

in himself, cut away the two youngest
and let the river take them, felt the sudden
terrible lightness of the line, swam hard

until they felt the shore under them. They made it
to the camps, where, safe and destroyed,
they could not move, as if their legs and feet

were filled with river water, muddied
and stinking. A story too heavy for parents
to carry alone, too heavy for travelers.

Look how it pours onto the page, soaking it,
running into the ink so that every story
is filled with this story.

2.
I've never seen that river. I imagine it braiding
itself fast over its stones, brown with the earth
it cuts through. Look how far it has run.

I hear it again: what it has cost
to come to this fire in this language,
to let a current of words take these children

again into unfamiliar ears. I see again
how we waded into war, that fast red river,
and cut away children. Those tiny bodies!—

The weight of ten rivers, moving forever
over our heads. Isn't it right that the story
circle back to its source? Isn't it we

who are drowning, wearing this necklace
of more and more stones—the watery
weight of these dead, our dead,

from mother to father, to river, to page.

Siciliana

after J.S. Bach, from Sonata No. 1 for solo violin, BWV 1001

We are in the middle of a story.
For me, it began like this:
a great-great-great grandmother,
whose name now is lost, said to her
granddaughter, Józka: *Go.*
There is nothing for you here.
And pressed a gold piece
into her hand.

Józka began the chromatic climb
that was her life, her story,
step by step through partitioned Poland
to the German port city of Danzig
to the American city of Baltimore
to the city of Chicago
where she made her home.

The story moved on. Have you been reading
the news? We are in a muddled wood now,
the middle of our story. We will have
to let belief illuminate our way.
You may scoff at this, you may say
freedom, dream, journey,
the lifted lamp beside a golden door,
all that, all that—
are motifs merely, motifs repeated,
but they made a song, I tell you,
and we believed.

Listen to my grandmothers.
Here is another line in their song:
a great-great grandmother
named Maria boarded a coffin ship
from Ireland and made it.

Safely in Ontario she hung pictures
of saints on her wall, saints
as examples of people who keep
the faith. And who are saints
but women with harrowing stories?

One of her nameless saints now hangs
         on my wall. She tells me:
         This is not the end of the story.

But it's gone wrong. Have you read the news?
Children are shuffled into cages. Troops wait
at the border. We don't know anymore
where this story will go.

Let me begin again: it seems only yesterday
my father leaned across the supper table: *Think
what you will give.* My mother looked
me in the eye: *Think
how lucky you are.* My grandmother
remembered in the evening: *O how they wept. O
how they wept.*

This story was given to me like a song,
like a stone worn and tumbled
by water, with oceans of feeling
and the oceans crossed to get here,
here a place big enough for dreams.

I know: this was not everyone's story.
You could say we were foolish
to believe it at all; underneath there were always
murder and despair, people in chains,
the smoking ruins of villages—and it's true.
There were, and more,
but still we believed.

Have you been reading the news?

We are too old now
to be called young.
And with the evidence mounting before us:
        beatings on video, audio
        of sobbing children, the testimony
        of survivors, bodies unearthed,
        and so on and so on

the question before us, as we come to ourselves
as in the middle of a dark wood
in the middle of our story:

        who are we
        what have we become

and

        by what alchemy
        might we remediate
        this poison?

Something must be said here
about belief, about the only thing remaining.
You may laugh.
They laughed too at Bach, at his
higher order, at his insistence
that a line could be found within harmonies,
that multiple voices could arrive
at a sweet understanding.

But this he knew: the end
of one line, one life
is not the end of the story.
Listen: there are continual
small arrivals, disharmonies resolved,
and still it goes on.

Let me begin again.
This is a poem about the middle
of the story, when song
moves us into difficulty
and there is no telling
where the story will go. Fear
is speaking.

The saint on my wall bows her head.
All she had was her belief. Did it save her?
She seems to be listening:
and here is a sweet note
undeniably sweet
and I think what courage there is
in melody carving its stairway out of the air.

The melody makes room for light,
makes an entire world
with love and trees and weather
and even
all the little insects blanketing

the grasses at night with their music,
in the darkness,
before daylight is certain,
because they were made to sing.

After a Line by Barry Lopez

…you are able to stake your life, again, in what you dream.
—*Barry Lopez*

Because the life is richest near the seams
the fisher moves toward moving water.
She stakes her life, again, in what she dreams.

Oh, easy enough to say—but the beam
of my attention and my courage often falter,
or my life is full—bursting, even, at the seams

with junk, administrivia, things we deem
important, but which hardly matter.
Can I stake my life again? My dreams

need re-imagining,—poor shadows!—gleam
in odd and unexpected corners, clatter
up in conversation, startle me. The seams

of What's-Supposed-To-Be look sewn up, seem
fixed and unassailable. How can I batter
at my life and live? I'm slow to give my dreams

the upper hand, but look, like salmon, they teem
and push, determined. They thrash in moving water.
They remember life is richest near the seams.
I must stake my life, again, in what I dream.

V.

What Moves, What Changes

A poem, like water, is hard to track
underground. Nobody really knows

when you put something into the water
where it will go, where it will end up.

Deep underground, large plates still move—
the molten bones of the planet.

Water finds its way around and through
like tides of blood moving unseen in the body.

Like a poem growing under the skin,
the swelling, the passing of dis-ease,

the dog of the mind circling in its shifting bed.

Asthma Attack

It's like a dance scene, a ball
in a Jane Austen story with lines
of dancers bowing and changing

hands. What is it about dances—
everything that's supposed to happen
happens. The ones who've been wary

are smiling at each other and offering
their arms. The red blood cells
look trim and fine in their regular

shapes, the oxygen keeps coming in
in pairs, clean and light in their airy
Regency dresses, and they meet,

they bow, they keep matching up,
stepping delicately around each other,
spinning around the alveolus

that's lit by a chandelier, and what
amazes you every breath is how
every single dancer knows the steps

and it occurs to you that this dance
has been going on since fish stepped
on shore, or even earlier, because

fish, don't they, and other creatures,
use oxygen, and you make a note
to look up the time period of Darwin's

theories though you're pretty sure
that Austen predates Darwin—just think
what Austen would have done

with Darwin's ideas!—and wouldn't
that be a dance to see those two
geniuses meet and bow to each other

as the dance goes on and now you
don't see the individuals so much
as the lovely rhythm, the pulse

of comings and goings and
the chandelier glows and there
are hundreds of millions of alveoli

just like this one all over the palace
but suddenly the light seems
                    to dim
and falter
                    and what's supposed

to be happening, isn't, and wait, there
it is again, the music, and a few steps
but the light stutters and the partners are

uncertain, scuttling, some red blood cells
make off with oxygen but
                    others are left

empty-handed and the Alveolus fills

with blue, there's more blue coming in

and the dance hall is closing, the lights
flashing on and off and you can't move,

you are locked inside that alveolus
and at the same time you are stepping

around outside with your hand on

the boulder that is your chest, bowing,
unsure, trying to restart,
                         trying to draw in

what's been flowing since you were a fish,

since you were pulled into air, wailing.

Mitosis

Arrested mid-split,
sliced and stained,
laid between layers
of glass, the purpled
spindles reach around
the chromosomes
and pull. This is how
it must be—the matched
homologous pairs,
which once were one,
now bent over double
as they are wrenched
apart.

Strange, the silence
of anguish under glass.
Like stained windows
in a church—bloodied
saints calling, reaching
out their palms.

How we keep becoming:
chromatin gathered into
thread—*Mit(os)*
from the ancient Greeks,
who were always
weaving, weren't they,
things that come apart.

The separated pairs
are dragged to the far ends
and held there like fighters,
like lovers torn, while
the cell walls close,
making two from one.

It gets confusing—
what is one, what
is the other.

Like, I had a father
once. When he left
his body, we were still

holding him with our
fingers, these spindles.
Or everything inside,
all the unseen silent
tearings—sometimes
I feel the pull
in my throat.

Look, I was cut, here
on my palm; now
it is healed. Think
what it took.

Matins

1.
My brother stands at the east window
by his bed, reading a stack of newspapers.

I'm at the kitchen table, stringing words together
like beads, letting them roll and softly clink

in my hands, on my lips. Far away, my mother cuts
clippings to mail, our weekly prayerbook.

Dutiful mother! She has given two children
to the Church of Words.

2.
Irish monks sat in the sun of a morning,
on the ground in the doorways of their stone huts,

while they transcribed the Word, illumined
each page—the gifts they left behind

for us to read, like bread taken into the body,
burned into light and heat, the kind of thing

we use rays of light to indicate—a shining,
the patina on a vessel often used.

3.
All those voices, all those hands, making
books for us to eat. Let us receive

these gifts, let words course through us,
let us leave behind only ashes,

inky prints on the doors, on the light
switches, signs that say: We were here.

We were writing. We were reading.

Unfinished

after the Golem of Prague

Golem, you called me. *Unfinished.* Your pet
project, your man-in-progress. So I was, and willing
enough to do your bidding. It was you,

Rabbi, who fashioned me from the clay
of the river Vltava, strong and fearsome,
to protect the people from pogroms. And it was you

who punished me, who took the name of God
out of my mouth. Because I shamed you?
You played Creator, but I asked the question

that you, the learned man, could not, cannot answer:

> *What should I do,*
> *what should We do,*
> *when Night falls?*

Even now the names pile and jostle
in the Pinkas Synagogue, clamoring for the eye of God.
And who has an answer for them?

Teacher, you are long gone, dust under the earth.
It is I who have lived on to watch history repeat,
to see how things change and do not change.

I am tired. I ask you, if you wanted to be rid
of me, why not return me to dust? No, you wanted
to know: *What makes a man a man?*

What does God know?

Loew, foolish man, locking me upstairs. Surely
you saw, when the Nazis came, everyone looked
up. There I was. People searching for God

found only monsters, unfinished men.

On the eve of a remembered slaughter

the President is speaking in my kitchen. His voice
is an intelligence, a steadiness of sound. I'm at the table
grading papers. My little dog lays his nose
on my knee, nudges it into my palm. He wants
to be assured. It is evening, but my clock beeps
on the counter and the young jay outside answers
with its own alarm. Everyone on the radio
has stopped talking to listen to the President.
He is talking about Syria, saying, listen, we all
must think this over. If we will bring peace
into the world. The dog takes my wrist in his teeth
and pulls my hand down so I will pet him.
Someone once told me I should never let
a dog touch me with his mouth but I have learned
that a dog's mouth is his hand. I'm grading papers,
writing comments to show I've read these young
stories, turned them over in my hands, pressed a little
at key spots. The dog retreats three feet and huffs at me, trying
to speak. His huffing blooms into barking. The President
is addressing the small part of the nation gathered
in my kitchen. We are not far from each other.
The dog shouts at me. The jay screams. How easy
it is to answer alarm with alarm. All over
the country we are waking into the anniversary
of the Towers falling, that great cry,
which was preceded by other, myriad cries.
We all are learning to listen. The dogs run
outside for yard-to-yard dog gossip. They add
their voices, stick out their chests, trot importantly
around the yard's perimeter, then duck
back in to nuzzle me. They love to stay close,
no matter my clumsiness in their language.

—September 10, 2013

Notes from the Land of Song

Across the road, the neighbor has brought his cows down
from the far pasture. They're grazing close to the barn, in sight
of their calves, who've been separated from the dams

for weeks now, living in a small paddock of their own.
All day the cows call to their calves, beginning before
first light. All day the calves answer them: You are mine,

you are mine. On this side of the road, the orphaned calf
lifts his head to listen. His mother was gone before he learned
her voice, before he found his own. He rarely speaks.

I am thinking of my own country: thousands of children held
in cages, shuffled under cover of night to new holding pens, toddlers
forced to appear alone before a judge. At this moment,

somewhere a tiny child sobs, or has fallen dead still. Somewhere
her parents are keening. Somewhere a banker, a realtor, a fence maker
is dining out, lifting a glass of good wine to his lips. How

can you find a missing child on an entire continent? Ah. Ah.

I'm standing in Ireland. In the language that my own people lost
I would say that the sadness is on me. All around is the weight
of history, people who know what it is to be starved out,

to be torn from their own. So much is too painful to speak of.
A man tells me, "Whatever else they took from us,
they couldn't take what was in here," and taps his brow, speaking

of poetry, speaking of song. Those lost children—how long
before their stories grind to a private silence? I wish for them
a song in every language. The orphaned calf and I listen

at the fence, to the calling across the road, the repeated
and essential note of belonging:

You.
You.
You.
You.

—*West Moveen*

Meanwhile

bombs fall on Ukraine, shattering everything
carefully made, frightening the animals, turning

parents into cloaks over children. The old
flee on the backs of younger men, picking

their way across broken bridges. Once they sat
in quiet houses. They gazed out

polished windows at trees and birds,
watched for spring. Outside my window

the white pine grows a foot every year.
It was taken from the woods by a friend,

who saw it hemmed in and struggling. Now
it grows fat and round. Once I found

a baby robin deep in its branches, stashed
there by a watchful parent while she

foraged. We shelter each other. Where
we are planted is pure chance.

For all we know, the trees of Ukraine,
who have no shelter, who appear in photos

halved, beheaded, scorched and jagged,
are crying out, their voices carried

by westerly winds all the way round
the world. For all I know, the trees

I live under feel tremors through their toes
in the earth, shudder for distant sisters.

For all I know, their rising sap catches
in their riverine throats.

Namaste

The question was, are rocks alive? I was a farmer
visiting New York City, gathering other perspectives.

John made pancakes for his friends for brunch. He'd already
shown me the roof, where he looked out over the fields

of buildings, water towers as blackened
and singular as trees. I didn't mention my delight

in the glow-in-the-dark stars on my pajamas
to the rocket scientist, but sought his opinion

on the practices of certain farmers: their belief
that distant cosmic influences could alter

compost. Yes, he said, it could be.
Then there was the Japanese custom of tying

white rope around objects—boulders and trees—
thought to be animated by spirit. I hoped

the sculptor could tell us something about the life
in rock, but he could only mumble from inside

his weathered face. Could stones be like this,
impervious but conducting some kind of light?

I thought of bees: by the time you can catch
up with a bee trapped indoors, it is in despair,

exhausted, trembling at the edge of a window
it cannot understand. Despite the light,

it cannot see. Once a man showed me
how, when carrying flowers to a lover,

one should tip the heads downward, to spare
the fragile stems. People, of course,

should raise their lovely heads. Heads
as sweetly shaped as lifted stones.

NOTES

"After A Line by Barry Lopez"

- Epigraph from Barry Lopez's *Arctic Dreams*

- A seam or crease in a river is created where slower and faster currents meet—created by boulders or debris, or where a back eddy meets the main current. Salmon use seams to slip in and out of the main current on their way upstream, thereby conserving energy.

"Dung Beetles"

- A study covered in *Current Biology* reports that dung beetles orient themselves using the light of the Milky Way. The study included, as a last confirming step, putting little cardboard hats on the beetles to block their view of the sky.

"Inquiry"

- "How's your water? Is it clean?" was shouted at Michigan Governor Rick Snyder in an Ann Arbor restaurant, in reference to the Flint water crisis. The reported silence of other patrons interested me.

- "Apparently it's going to be a thing now.": from Michigan Department of Environmental Quality spokesperson Karen Tommasulo's internal email dismissing media inquiries and Flint residents' concerns.

"Unfinished"

- The Golem is a man-like being, in Jewish folklore, made of clay or mud. The Golem of Prague was said to be created by the rabbi Judah Loew ben Bezalel to help protect the people from pogroms. He animated the Golem by putting a *shem* (a piece of paper inscribed with the word or name of God) into its mouth; he removed the shem, deactivating the Golem, on Friday evenings before Sabbath services. One Friday, the Rabbi forgot, and the Golem went on a rampage. The Rabbi eventually deactivated the Golem and stored it in the attic of the Old New Synagogue.

- Some 78,000 names of Bohemian and Moravian Jewish victims of the Shoah, or Holocaust, were inscribed in the 1940s on the walls of the Pinkas Synagogue in Prague.

"Notes from the Land of Song"

- An Gorta Mór, or the Great Hunger: the Irish famine of 1845-1849, during which an estimated 1-1.5 million people died of starvation or related disease. Another 1-2 million people emigrated. In some areas, deaths rose to 25% or even 38% of the population. Outside Ireland it is sometimes called the Potato Famine, because many people depended on the potato as their primary food source. However, there was plenty of food produced in Ireland during this time, which was exported to England under armed guard to pay absentee landlords.

- George Petrie described an "awful, unwonted silence, which during the Famine and subsequent years almost everywhere prevailed." He writes: "Of the old, who had still preserved the language, the songs and traditions of their race and their localities, but few survived ... The land of song was no longer tuneful; or, if a human sound met the traveller's ear, it was only that of the feeble and despairing wail for the dead." From *The Petrie Collection of the Ancient Music of Ireland*, published in 1855.

"Vagrants"

- A "vagrant" or an "accidental" is a biological term used for birds which are found far outside their normal range.

- Michigan Bean Queen: A long-time native of Michigan's Thumb.

- "Navigation gone gollywhompus. This actually happens," and "It's not the bird that's important here. It's how you feel about the bird." Jim Williams quoted in the April 14, 2015 *Minneapolis Star Tribune*.

ACKNOWLEDGMENTS

Thank you to the editors of the journals in which these poems first appeared:

Artful Dodge: "Vagrants"

Cold Mountain Review: "After Perfection," "The Snapper"

Dunes Review: "After a Line by Barry Lopez," "Corduroy Quilt," "On the Painting of a Geranium"

Feminist Quarterly Review: "Factory Job"

The Fourth River: "King Kong," "Namaste"

Hypertext: "I Want to Be Joe Manchin's Momma"

Juxtaprose: "Mitosis"

Michigan Poet: "Spring"

Nimrod: "Asthma Attack," "Cabbages," "Geopolitics, Stateside," "Meanwhile," "On the eve of a remembered slaughter," "Stolen Code," "What Moves, What Changes"

Split This Rock: "River, Page"

Waxwing: "Shame and Something Else"

The poem "Inquiry" was first published on the author's website.

The poem "Siciliana" was written for *Bach and the Poets: Slow Dancing*, an ekphrastic project by violist Christine Rutledge and performed October 30, 2019, at the Interlochen Center for the Arts, Interlochen, Michigan.

The following poems were published in the chapbook *Trees and Other Creatures* (Alice Greene & Co., 2021): "The Snapper," "Shame and Something Else," "Dung Beetles," "On the eve of a remembered slaughter," and "Namaste."

* * *

My thanks to the Lynch and Sons Fund for the Arts, whose 2018 Moveen Poetry Prize provided the time and place to work on this book.

The cover photo of a baby snapping turtle was taken by Ranger D. Archuleta at the Sleeping Bear Dunes National Lakeshore. My grateful thanks to the National Park Service staff for helping me to track down this photo, for the permission to use it, and for all of their work to steward this beautiful place.

Grateful thanks to the people at Cornerstone Press, including: Dr. Ross Tangedal, Eva Nielsen, Allison Lange, Sophie McPherson, Autumn Vine, Madison Schultz, and Ava Willett. From start to finish, I have felt this book was in good and caring hands.

Special thanks to Fleda Brown, Sheena Carey, Mark Jarman, Thomas Lynch, Anne-Marie Oomen, Jill Peek, Jennifer Steinorth, Alison Swan, Catherine Turnbull, Baron Wormser, and Jennifer Yeatts, who have seen and supported this work as it progressed. Thank you to Christine Rutledge, a creative and collaborative maestra. Thank you to Joan Gallagher Richmond for her cover design and to Allison Lange for making it real.

And my grateful thanks to the community of poets, writers, artists, and musicians who support and inspire me.

TERESA J. SCOLLON is a poet, essayist, editor, and educator. Her publications include poetry collections *Trees and Other Creatures* (2021) and *To Embroider the Ground with Prayer* (2012); the chapbook *Friday Nights the Whole Town Goes to the Basketball Game* (2009); and poems and essays in journals. Her work is included in *Poetry in Michigan/Michigan in Poetry* from New Issues Press, and in *Elemental*, a 2018 anthology of essays about Michigan. She is a National Endowment for the Arts Fellow; alumna and past Writer-in-Residence at Interlochen Arts Academy; a past recipient of a fellowship from Western Michigan University's Prague Summer Program, and the winner of the 2018 Moveen Prize in Poetry. A native of Michigan's Thumb, Teresa teaches the North Ed Writers Studio (formerly Front Street Writers) program for high school students at the Northwest Education Services Career Tech in Traverse City, Michigan.

www.ingramcontent.com/pod-product-compliance
Lightning Source LLC
Chambersburg PA
CBHW050857150626
46549CB00013B/2725

9 7 8 1 9 6 0 3 2 9 8 9 9